Managing crowds safely

HSE BOOKS

HSG154

© Crown copyright 2000
Applications for reproduction should be made in writing to: Copyright Unit, Her Majesty's Stationery Office, St Clements House, 2-16 Colegate, Norwich NR3 1BQ

First published 1996
Second edition 2000

ISBN 0 7176 1834 X

This guidance is issued by the Health and Safety Executive. Following the guidance is not compulsory and you are free to take other action. But if you do follow the guidance you will normally be doing enough to comply with the law. Health and safety inspectors seek to secure compliance with the law and may refer to this guidance as illustrating good practice.

HSE thanks those who contributed to producing this guidance and the following who provided photographs: NEC, Edinburgh Fringe Festival, Shakespeare's Globe Theatre, Glastonbury Festival, National Pictures.

Contents

Introduction

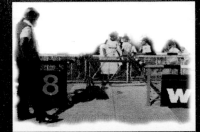

The guide and its aims

1   Crowds are unavoidable occurrences of everyday life; problems in their safe management are not. This guide aims to provide practical guidance to help those organising events to manage crowd safety in a systematic way. It does not specify a particular way of achieving crowd safety, but sets out a general approach.

2   Although primarily aimed at organisers who have overall responsibility for the event, the guide will be of use to others involved in the event, such as venue staff and contractors.

3   There is potential for minor or major injury occurring through the dynamics of crowd behaviour, as past tragedies have demonstrated. Measures should be taken by the organisers of events to ensure that there is effective and safe crowd management so that overcrowding does not occur.

4   Crowding occurs as a result of an excessively large number of people gathering in a specified area. Large numbers gather routinely in such places as shopping malls, train stations, bus stations etc. However, they also gather, often in greater density, where particular attractions or events are taking place, such as at sporting events, concerts, theatres, cinemas and festivals. At such events there may be greater risks to their safety.

5   This guidance addresses:

- events, both sporting and non-sporting, at football stadia and other sports grounds;

- events at sites not designed for the purpose such as parks or industrial units, eg a fair on a town common or a public air-show on an airfield; and

- events in streets or built-up areas, eg street fairs, carnival processions, New Year celebrations.

6   For the purpose of this publication, the 'organiser' is taken to be anyone who has prime responsibility for the event. The arrangements themselves may involve a number of people, depending upon the contractual arrangements under which the event is to be run.

7   In order to successfully run the event, organisers may employ staff or use volunteers. They may hire self-employed people (such as lighting managers) or contractors (for stewarding duties or erection of a temporary stand). They may also hire out plots for catering, merchandising or attractions, such as fairground rides.

8   The parties involved all have duties under health and safety legislation. The duties are outlined in the following paragraphs and further details are given in the Appendix. Close liaison and strong communication are

essential in ensuring that health and safety responsibilities for the event are identified, assigned and adhered to. These include responsibility for crowd safety.

9   If, as an event organiser, you are in charge of a business or organisation, you will have general duties under the Health and Safety at Work etc Act 1974 (HSW Act)[1] to ensure that risks to people's health and safety arising from work activities, including members of the public, self-employed persons, volunteers and contractors, are properly controlled. You may allocate elements of the organisation of your event to others, eg event stewards provided by a contractor, but you will retain overall responsibility for ensuring the safety of the visiting crowds.

10   Contractors and subcontractors, as employers, have duties under the HSW Act to ensure the health and safety of members of the public, who may be affected by their undertaking. For example, a contractor will need to ensure that the barriers they are erecting will not fall over and cause injury to the crowd. The self-employed have similar duties.

11   The Management of Health and Safety at Work Regulations 1999 (the MHSW Regulations)[2] generally make more explicit what employers and the self-employed are required to do to manage health and safety law under the HSW Act. The MHSW Regulations set out key steps to ensure that activities, including events, are managed safely.

12   The information in this guide expands on the chapter on crowd management in *The event safety guide*,[3] which covers many other issues for organisers to consider when staging an event.

Section summary

The following sections provide advice that should help you run a safe and successful event. They should also help meet your legal obligations to protect the audience and staff.

Planning

Describes important milestones in planning your event. A safe and trouble-free event requires good planning from an early stage.

You need to ensure that your precautions to manage crowds are adequate and appropriate for the expected number and type of visitor. Planning involves gathering background information to enable both thinking ahead and assessing risks, and time to develop or modify plans.

Assessing risks

Describes how to systematically identify hazards which could affect crowd safety, eg surging and swaying, estimate the size of the problems and decide what you need to do to address the problems. This process is known as risk assessment, which involves the identification and assessment of risks to crowd safety within a venue and the development of steps required to minimise them. Depending upon the outcome of the risk assessment, plans may be modified.

Putting precautions in place

Gives examples of practical precautions that can be taken to address potential hazards identified through your risk assessment. Describes arrangements for the selection and training of staff.

Emergency planning and procedures

Sets out issues to consider when planning for the safe management of crowds in the event of an emergency, eg due to fire or bomb threat. Such plans are very important as an emergency could involve rapid, large-scale movement of people with potential for overcrowding.

Communication

Describes importance of good communication and gives practical examples. Effective communication is particularly important in the safe management of crowds.

Provision of clear, unambiguous information to visitors can help prevent dangerous situations arising. Good communication between staff assists a rapid and appropriate response if problems arise.

Monitoring crowds

Covers the actions involved in implementing your plans and checking to make sure they have been implemented correctly. Where crowd activity may develop into hazardous overcrowding, monitoring should be in place to identify potential problems and quickly sort them out. This section gives examples of practical approaches to crowd monitoring.

Review

Sets out ways to formally review the crowd safety system of your event and explains the need to do so. Reviews can be a debrief after an event, part of an investigation following a crowd-related incident, or scheduled routine examination. Subsequently, plans can be modified and future plans updated according to the outcome of your review. Reviewing one-off events or regular review of safety measures at your venue provides important feedback for improving crowd safety standards and checking that your precautions continue to be appropriate.

Planning

13 Good planning from an early stage will help you run your event safely. You need to allow sufficient time to gather information, consult and obtain advice and put in place effective precautions to manage crowd safety. The safe running of your event should be given equal priority to other business aims.

14 It is important to involve staff representing different facets of the event, eg technical staff, security, merchandise. Where appropriate, representatives of relevant outside bodies, such as local authorities and emergency services, should be brought into the planning process.

15 To minimise the risk of overcrowding, you need to consider the activities, movement and dynamics of the crowd at various parts within the venue, at the entrance and exits, on the pedestrian routes to and from the venue and at the transport and parking facilities.

First steps

16 As an early priority, you need to establish that you can manage crowd safety for the type of event and at the venue you have chosen. An acceptable level of crowd density varies according to the venue. A preliminary walk around your proposed venue, carrying out a visual inspection, is essential to find out both the suitability and the acceptable level of crowd density for your event. Key issues to consider at this stage are considered below.

Expected turnout

17 When forecasting your expected turnout, you may find it helpful to consider:

- attendance on previous occasions;

- numbers visiting similar events;

- proposed level of publicity;

- advance ticket sales;

- the effect of Bank Holidays, school holidays or good/bad weather;

- whether some days are going to be particularly busy, eg first or final days;

- whether any extra visitors will attend special attractions taking place at the event; and

- allowance for unexpectedly large numbers of people turning up.

Types of visitor

18 The nature of the visiting crowd will influence your planning and choice of venue. Children, people with special needs and the elderly need special consideration. People frequently attend events as a family or small group and will not want to get separated or leave each other, particularly in emergency situations.

19 Performers can have a significant influence on crowd mood and behaviour, eg by jumping into the crowd or throwing items into it, or by calming the crowd, if pushing or surging starts to occur. Several acts/performances at an event may attract different groups of people, resulting in considerable crowd movement. For example, where one particular performer has a large or enthusiastic following, the audience may suddenly surge forward and crushing could result.

20 Crushing, trampling and suffocation are all potential hazards that can arise from the dynamics of crowd movement. To help avoid harm from crowd surges etc, ensure that crowd behaviour and movement are monitored effectively, eg by placing stewards/CCTV at suitable vantage points. All staff should know their precise roles in crowd monitoring and who has the authority to take immediate action (eg by stopping the event) if people are at risk.

Getting to and from the venue

21 Plan your transport management arrangements well in advance, eg:

- Where are the nearest bus and train stations located and will existing timetables be adequate?

- Where are the local car and coach parks?

- Is existing parking adequate?

- Is the layout of roads and pedestrian routes to the venue adequate to deal with the expected turnout?

- Are there any other venues nearby (especially those which may affect the crowding situation at your event)?

- Is any construction work being carried out or proposed in the area? Roadworks could delay the arrival of crowds and lead to a late rush.

Venue suitability

22 Ensure that the maximum capacity of the venue is established. This is to allow:

- management of the crowd and help in eliminating overcrowding in terms of overall number of people in the venue;

- safe entrance and exit; and

- safe exit of people in an emergency.

Ensure staff are briefed thoroughly

23 The maximum capacity should be calculated with reference to four factors:

- the time it takes to get into the venue;

- the time it takes to get out of the venue;

- emergency evacuation time; and

- accommodation capacity.

Each of these capacities is likely to give a different figure. The safe capacity is the lowest of the four.

24 When calculating capacity, ensure that allowance is made for areas taken up by facilities such as food and merchandising stalls, temporary structures etc as people cannot use these areas. Areas where there is no easy access to view the main attraction(s) should also be identified. Whatever the results of the calculation, the capacity should never exceed the limit calculated for means of escape purposes. (More guidance on this point can be found in the first chapter of the Stationery Office publication *Guide to safety at sports grounds*.)[4]

25 Consider the distribution of crowds and how this might affect permissible capacity. Are the following adequate for your proposed event?

- Capacity of the venue

- Entrances and exits

- Means of escape in event of emergency

- Provision for people with special needs

- Maintenance of venue and equipment (eg turnstiles)

- Facilities such as toilets and information points

- Access to first-aid facilities

- Suitable means of access/exit for emergency services

- Provision for adverse weather conditions

- Arrangements in place to ensure crowd safety if maintenance or construction work is being carried out in the venue

26 The amount of space available to the audience is an important factor to consider. For example, more space may be needed at a pop concert than a sporting event due to the time people will be in the venue. See the checklist after paragraph 61.

Excess arrivals

27 If there is any possibility that the number of people arriving at the venue will come near to or exceed the overall capacity of the venue, you will need:

- a system for restricting the number of people who arrive at the venue as well as those who enter it. This demands close liaison with the police and transport operators at the planning stage and during the lead-in period before the event; and

- arrangements for closely monitoring the numbers of people arriving.

28 You could:

- make the event 'all-ticket', even if it's free;

- plan the advertising campaign to emphasise that it's all-ticket only;

- include in the advertising that the ticket-only rule will be strictly enforced;

- discuss with the police how crowds could be redirected before reaching the venue;

- discuss with the transport operators the possibility of announcements at stations, advising the public of crowd problems at the venue; and

- use local radio to advise on the current situation at the venue.

Previous information collected

29 You could refer to:

- experience of similar venues or events;

- problems raised at previous event debriefings;

- reports of previous incidents;

- experience of running events at a similar season/time of day; and

- experience of previous delays.

30 Seeking advice from relevant and experienced parties will help you obtain the information you require. It is advisable, if practical, to visit other venues holding similar events to obtain the relevant information. In some venues the requirements of the local authority and the fire authority will determine key precautions you need to take. Relevant parties include:

- the owner of the venue where you are proposing to hold your event;

- the local authority, for example licensing, environmental health and emergency planning departments;

- police and other emergency services;

- transport operators or management of nearby transport venues;

- management of adjoining or adjacent public venues;

- local residents or their representatives, particularly if you are organising an event such as a carnival parade that goes through their residential area;

- others providing services for the event (eg stewarding, first-aid and welfare organisations and merchandising) and any experts giving advice, eg on the structural stability of a proposed temporary stand; and

- other subcontractors, eg a structures production manager.

TS OFF TO

HANNAH
THE
SPANNER

Getting organised

31 Once the decision to proceed with your event is made, start by holding regular event planning meetings, bringing together all the main interested parties. Provide relevant information - see the 'Checklist for strategic project planning' at the end of this section.

32 From an early stage, ensure that clearly defined roles and responsibilities exist in relation to crowd safety, addressing both normal and emergency situations. Whatever management structure you choose, you will need to decide who is responsible for the various safety duties, making sure there are no gaps and ensuring everyone understands their own responsibilities. If a number of people are involved, there will need to be close liaison and good communication between them. Consider all other related staff or developments and external bodies or organisations who could at some point be involved in crowd management at the event.

33 It is important that meetings, and what has been agreed between various parties, have been clearly documented to avoid unnecessary confusion and misunderstanding.

34 An event controller (safety officer) should be appointed by the event organiser to co-ordinate all aspects of safety relative to the event. Although this person must be able to act without reference to others, that appointment does not remove the responsibility of the event organiser. The event controller must have final control over all subcontractors, stewards etc, although their control may be via intermediaries.

35 As an organiser, you have primary responsibility for the safety of the crowd. However, you may need to consider whether it would be appropriate to appoint a senior member of staff to take overall responsibility for crowd management when the venue is open to the public. Always ensure there is someone with the authority to act in their place if this person is unavailable.

36 If you are an employer, you have a legal duty under the MHSW Regulations to appoint one or more competent persons to assist you with your health and safety duties. You should look to appoint competent person(s), where they exist, from among your employees in preference to external sources of competent advice and assistance. If you are a sole trader or member of a partnership, you may appoint yourself (or other partners), so long as you (or they) are competent. You can use external sources of competent advice and assistance if no internal source exists. Indeed, in these circumstances you would need to appoint a competent person from outside your organisation in order to comply with the law.

37 The person appointed could provide assistance in the following ways:

- expert advice on crowd management and venue suitability for input to the planning process;

- inspection of the venue and developing procedures for managing the crowds; and

- investigation of incidents relating to crowding.

38 The person appointed would need to ensure that there are enough staff with the required skills to carry out crowd management duties during both normal and emergency situations. Staff need to be carefully selected and trained to ensure that they can fulfil their defined roles and responsibilities in relation to crowd safety. Training is important as overcrowding can develop extremely quickly and requires a rapid response from staff.

39 Where crowd management duties are subcontracted (eg to a private stewarding company) you should ensure that the contractor's staff are competent and have received training appropriate to their responsibilities.

Keeping records

40 If you employ five or more people, you have a legal duty to produce several written documents or records (see the Appendix for further details). These include your health and safety policy and significant findings of risk assessments.

41 It is recommended that records are also kept of contingency plans, staff training/job descriptions, and checks/inspections of sites and structures.

Crowd behaviour

42 Research has highlighted several important factors which influence the way crowds behave. These factors may affect the types of precautions you put in place to ensure crowd safety and need to be considered during your event planning.

The crowd's goals and objectives

43 This is very often one of the most important factors affecting how people behave. It may affect, for example, when people choose to arrive and leave, which routes they choose to take, where people want to gather etc.

44 For example, people may:

- arrive early to gain vantage points from where to watch the event. Once there, they may be reluctant to move away, even if asked to do so;

- park illegally, obstructing access for emergency vehicles, so that they can make a quick getaway;

- wait for friends/family at or near exits and obstruct the flow of people;

- choose to use the most direct or quickest route rather than follow a designated one; or

- quickly change direction, eg fans leaving a music concert early may rush back if they hear a favourite song during the encore.

The crowd's knowledge and experience

45 People who are unfamiliar with the event or venue generally require more assistance and direction. They tend to follow the crowds, use the main routes and gather at the same accommodation areas. This can lead to an uneven distribution of people. They may not be aware of alternative routes or entrances which they could use to reduce congestion. Those who are familiar with the venue may use short cuts, rather than follow the directional signs.

46 Visitors may be unaware of the locations of emergency exits. So they will choose to use those routes or exits with which they are familiar or which are the most obvious, rather than those which are closest or give the quickest evacuation time.

47 You can improve site familiarity with details on the back of tickets, plans of the venue strategically placed inside and out, and through good use of signs.

48 It is important to note that venues and outdoor sites can look very different in the light and the dark. People may become disorientated if they arrive in the light and depart in the dark.

The crowd's expectations

49 Prior expectations are likely to have a significant impact upon people's reactions under certain circumstances:

- Visitors might regard some routes and entry points as the 'formal' or main access to the event. Perhaps such a route is the most direct between the parking area and the part of the venue that they want to visit. It might be wider and resemble the main route with adjacent facilities such as toilets and stalls.

- Where smoke or similar effects are part of an event (eg a fireworks display, dry ice effects at a pop concert), people are likely to respond more slowly to the presence of smoke generated by a fire hazard.

50 You need to consider if certain groups of people will exhibit undesirable behaviour. Further precautions may be necessary, for example the use of barriers to set up a diversion, or the use of staff to direct flows of crowd traffic.

51 You may be able to use certain forms of behaviour to your advantage. For example, once an orderly queue is set up, it tends to attract people and introduce some order into crowd patterns.

The crowd's mental and emotional conditions

52 People's emotions, such as excitement, desperation, aggression, hysteria etc, may affect their behaviour. For example, people who are eager to gain entry may surge towards the doors when they are opened. Those not satisfied with the quality of a performance or outcome of a sporting fixture may become aggressive, offensive and unco-operative.

Collective behaviour

53 The behaviour of individuals in a crowd can be influenced by the things they see others doing. The unauthorised actions of a few people can result in larger numbers following their example. Individuals within a crowd may carry out actions which they would not perform if they were on their own. For example, the frustration of excessive crowding, queuing or delays may result in incidents such as climbing of barriers which could lead to overcrowding in another area.

54 If safety rules are not visibly enforced, or crowd control is not maintained, the spread of non-compliant behaviour can have a serious impact on crowd safety. For example, if a few people gain entry to a prohibited area by climbing over or under a barrier, others may follow suit if the response from those controlling the crowd is slow, weak, or non-existent. The resulting uncontrolled crowd flow may lead to overcrowding and other related hazards.

55 In the early stages of an emergency situation, crowd behaviour can be influenced by individuals who appear to be 'experts' or know what to do. An individual or group of people taking decisive action (eg leaving a nearby exit, outwardly dismissing a warning as a false alarm) can trigger a widespread response among the crowd. Members of staff might be allocated to evacuate a venue or another area.

Information

56 In general, people look for clear, unambiguous information and indicators on expected rules of behaviour to help them decide how to act, eg to find out if a particular door is an entrance, an exit, or both, or whether they can drink or smoke in the venue. If such information and instructions are not provided, people will form their own rules based on past experience and the observed behaviour of others, such as joining a queue, parking on access routes, taking short cuts etc.

Good use of signs and public address systems is therefore extremely important.

57 Providing visual and audible information (eg warnings, advice, directions, instructions) is of vital importance during an emergency when the situation can be confusing and unfamiliar. Figures of authority (eg promoter, steward, firefighter) are likely to be listened to and obeyed in an emergency. For this reason, such people should always wear easily identifiable clothes/colours.

Relationships between staff and the public

58 People are more likely to be in a relaxed and contented frame of mind if they are effectively managed and the venue is comfortable and pleasant, with adequate facilities, such as toilets, food, drink and information points. People are more likely to comply with instructions if good relations are maintained between venue staff and the public. Therefore, it is imperative that information is effectively communicated to them through the staff, so that confusion or causes for complaint are avoided.

59 The 'attitude' of the predicted audience may be different to that expected. For example, security searches or ticket checks which you might decide to do may be contrary to the ticket holders' expectations. This could have the potential for the development of ill feeling, which could result in public order problems.

The next steps

60 Identify possible hazards that could harm people attending or involved in your event. Variation in crowd behaviour means there is often more than one way to tackle a particular hazard. For example, in order to ensure an early and effective response in an evacuation, where panic may be a feature, measures might be taken to improve the quality and clarity of information that is both broadcasted over the public address system and displayed through the use of signs. Such measures would enhance the role of staff in directing or leading people out of the venue and aid the staff in maintaining as much calm as possible.

61 Looking systematically at the hazards associated with your event will help you put in place effective precautions to ensure crowd safety. The following sections suggest ways of doing this.

Checklist for venue suitability

- Are public transport arrangements to and from the site adequate to deal with expected numbers of visitors and for periods of peak demand?

- Are arrangements for vehicle parking and pedestrian approach to the venue adequate?

- Are there sufficient entrances, spaces and routes (ie roads, gangways, walkways, stairs etc) inside and outside the venue to cope with the expected numbers and are they adequate to cope if people arrive in sudden masses rather than an even flow?

- Are precautions in place to deal with possible crowd pressure at the entrances and exits to the venue?

- Will the sound quality be suitable for the event, eg to avoid crowding at the front of the stage?

- Has the overall capacity of the venue been established and precautions put in place to prevent over-capacity?

- Have you checked the trouble spots? For example:

  - routes which become narrow or areas in which people could congregate, as these may cause congestion;

  - bottlenecks such as stairs, escalators and tunnels or bridges;

  - areas where people queue, such as pay desks and information points; or

  - popular stalls, attractions or exhibition and refreshment areas.

- Is the safety of vulnerable groups (eg children, people with special needs and the elderly) addressed?

- Are the means of escape adequate in event of an emergency?

- Has adequate access been provided for the emergency services?

- Have particular hazards arising from the venue been taken into account, eg has drowning been considered as a hazard at water events or events adjacent to water?

Is the venue properly maintained in a safe condition, eg floors, stairways and lighting?

Have litter and combustible materials been removed to safe storage or disposed of?

Is emergency equipment, eg firefighting equipment, emergency lighting, fire alarms, smoke alarms, public address and other communication systems, properly maintained and in good working order?

Are fire exits unlocked, and are escape routes unobstructed and free from hazardous and combustible materials?

Are all direction and information signs in place and clearly legible?

Checklist for strategic project planning

Plans and drawings:

- production of scaled plans of site or venue with temporary installations plotted onto the drawing to be distributed to key personnel.

Meetings calendar:

- details of pre-production, during performance and post-production (review) meetings.

Inspection calendar:

- details of site suitability survey;

- inspections during build; and

- inspections during performance.

Legal calendar:

- details of licences, certificates, concerts and notifications required by legislation.

Assessing risks

General principles of risk assessment

62 Look carefully at what you are proposing to do and identify hazards, ie those things that could harm the people involved or attending. You are required by law to assess what precautions you need to take to prevent harm. This process is referred to as risk assessment. Risk is the chance, high or low, that somebody will be harmed by the hazard.

63 Risk assessment is a legal requirement under the MHSW Regulations. Regulation 3 requires all employers and the self-employed (including those who organise events) to assess the risks to workers and anyone else, for example members of the public attending an event, who may be affected by work activities being undertaken. Both the HSW Act and regulations covering particular hazards require that appropriate preventive and protective measures should be taken in the light of the risks identified.

64 Your risk assessment needs to examine all aspects of your event, including transport to and from the event. You need to think about incidents that could occur, even if they seem unlikely, eg a visitor collapsing from heat exhaustion or a larger scale emergency such as a fire, bomb threat or stand collapse. You also need to carefully evaluate all places where there may be potential for high crowd density and subsequent crushing, eg queuing areas at the venue entrance.

65 During early planning, identify people who have the right competence and knowledge to contribute to the risk assessment process. The important things you need to decide are whether a hazard is significant, and whether you have dealt with it satisfactorily through taking the relevant precautions, so that the risk is reduced or minimal.

66 HSE has developed a five step approach to risk assessment:

> **STEP 1:** Look for the hazards.

> **STEP 2:** Decide who might be harmed and how.

> **STEP 3:** Evaluate the risks and decide whether the existing precautions are adequate or whether more should be done.

> **STEP 4:** Record your findings.

> **STEP 5:** Review your assessment and revise it if necessary.

For more guidance on this, see the HSE publication *Five steps to risk assessment: A step by step guide to a safer and healthier workplace.*[5] The following paragraphs give advice on how you might carry out a risk assessment with examples relating to event organisation.

STEP 1 Look for the hazards

67 Consider all aspects of the proposed activity and look at what could reasonably be expected to cause harm. Ignore the trivial and concentrate on significant hazards which could result in serious harm or affect several people, eg funnelling of visitors at the venue entrance leading to congestion and crushing.

68 Speak to your staff about possible hazards - they may have noticed things that are not immediately obvious to you. It may be helpful to refer to previous information, eg post-event reports, incident reports or visitors' comments.

69 Consider hazards associated with the crowd and those presented by the venue. It is important to identify hazards that are not immediately apparent such as a hazard that arises due to the introduction of a new feature, eg the late addition of several market stalls at a venue may restrict access routes and lead to congestion.

Hazards presented by a crowd

- Crushing between people

- Crushing against fixed structures, such as barriers

- Trampling underfoot

- Surging, swaying or rushing

- Aggressive behaviour, particularly between groups of rival supporters

- Dangerous behaviour, such as climbing on equipment, running down steep slopes or throwing objects

Hazards presented by a venue

- Slipping or tripping due to inadequately lit areas or poorly maintained floors

- Moving vehicles sharing the same route as pedestrians

- People getting trapped, eg wheelchair users in a crowd

- Collapse of a structure, such as a fence or barrier, which falls onto the crowd

- People being pushed against objects, such as unguarded, hot cooking equipment on a food stall

- Objects, such as stalls, that obstruct movement and cause congestion during busy periods

- Crowd movements obstructed by people queuing

- Crossflows as people cut through the crowd to get to other areas, such as toilets

- Failure of equipment, such as turnstiles

- Sources of fire, such as cooking equipment

70 For the purpose of this guidance, aspects of activities are considered under five topics, listed below. You may find the topics helpful when looking for hazards and completing the rest of your risk assessment.

Nature of the event - Who will be attending and what is their expected behaviour? What might they do that could cause a problem?

Venue suitability - Is the venue adequate for ensuring the safety of people throughout the event?

Crowd management arrangements - Are arrangements adequate? For example, clear roles and responsibilities; command and communication structures in place; good co-operation and co-ordination throughout the organisation of the event; sufficient monitoring of crowds; provision of appropriate numbers of competent and trained staff.

Presence of hazardous items and substances - Your activity may involve the use and storage of items or substances which could pose a hazard to the crowd. In such circumstances, the relevant specific health and safety regulations should be observed.

'When things go wrong' - Think about how your activity could be disrupted and what new hazards could arise as a result of a disruption. An emergency, such as a serious fire, may call for an evacuation, thus introducing new hazards. Even a minor disruption, such as a train delay or cancellation, could turn into a significant hazard.

71 Identify the scenarios which could disrupt your activity, such as:

- emergency situations (eg fire, bomb threat, structural collapse, toxic release etc);

- accident (eg traffic accident, outside or within the venue);

- closure of part of the venue;

- closure of a nearby or related venue (eg the closure of an adjacent train station);

- delay or cancellation (eg late kick-off in a football match);

- disruption to the arrival/departure profile (eg severe traffic congestion on a main approach road);

- loss of services (eg power cut);

- public disorder;

Look for the hazards

- system or equipment failure (eg jammed door or gate, escalator stops); or

- weather (eg a sudden change of weather and adverse weather conditions such as too hot/cold, heavy rainfall/snowfall, high winds etc).

72 For the scenarios you have identified, consider the effect the disruption could have on people's behaviour, venue operation, crowd management and on the items or substances you are using. Then identify what new hazards may arise as a result. For example, a severe traffic problem due to roadworks on one of the main approach roads to the venue could lead to a last minute rush and congestion at the entrance to the venue.

STEP 2: Decide who might be harmed and how

73 In the case of major disruption, such as emergencies involving a major fire or bomb threat, detailed assessment of significant hazards is likely to be necessary. Managing such disruptions is dealt with in more detail in the 'Emergency planning and procedures' section.

74 The aim of this step is to find out what causes the hazards identified in Step 1, what dangers they could pose and who might be affected. Knowing the cause(s) could help you to decide later in the assessment process what actions are needed to get rid of the hazards. Thinking about the consequences and who might be harmed could help you to decide how to protect people against the harm.

How might people be harmed (what are the causes)?

75 You may have already found the immediate causes earlier on in Step 1. But don't stop there - there could be other causes that are equally important. It is worth emphasising again that a hazard could arise from a combination of factors, including the suitability of the venue, the crowd and their behaviour, the crowd management arrangements and the presence of hazardous items or substances.

76 Some causes may not be immediately obvious. Congestion, for example, could be the result of an object obstructing crowd flows, insufficient capacity or a pinch point (ie venue suitability), people assembling or waiting for others in the area (ie behaviour) and too many people being directed to use this area (ie crowd management). It could also be because of a problem elsewhere in the venue or what happens nearby, such as crowds leaving a nearby football match.

77 If the hazard is caused by people's behaviour, you also need to know why people behave in such a way (see paragraphs 42-59).

Who might be harmed?

78 Think about the consequences and who might be harmed. This could include anyone in the crowd or anyone exposed to overcrowded conditions for a prolonged period of time. You need to consider the number of people who may be affected. Also, ask yourself if the hazard could only harm the individuals directly involved or if others in the vicinity could be affected. Children, young people, people with special needs and the elderly are particularly vulnerable and need special consideration. Remember that your own staff and contractors could also be at risk, particularly those who might have to deal with a difficult situation.

Examples			
Hazard	People could trip on stairs within the venue	**Hazard**	People falling over as a result of crowd dynamics
Causes	People pushing their way through the crowd	**Causes**	Misjudgement of attraction's popularity
	Inadequate lighting in the area		Unexpected mass movement of audience
	Poor construction of stairs		Non-management of aggressive/irresponsible behaviour by crowd
Who might be harmed	People being pushed could fall down the stairs. They could be trampled on	**Who might be harmed**	Those within the crowd and at the edge of 'wave'
	Young and old people are particularly vulnerable		

STEP 3: Evaluate the risks and decide whether the existing precautions are adequate or whether more should be done

Evaluate the risks

79 The aim is to decide for each significant hazard how much risk still remains after the existing precautions have been taken into account. The findings will enable you to establish how important the hazards are and

prioritise actions you need to take to control them.

80 Risk reflects the likelihood that harm from a particular hazard will occur and the potential severity of that harm. To evaluate the risk you need to estimate the likelihood and the severity.

81 When estimating likelihood, it is important that you consider how likely the hazard is to occur and to cause harm. This is because not all hazards cause harm all the

Check existing precautions

Hold training sessions

28

time. For example, crossflows and obstructions do not normally give rise to a significant problem, unless they take place in a busy area.

82 Severity is a consideration of the extent of possible injuries, ranging from little real harm to an individual to multiple deaths. When estimating severity, you need to take into account the circumstances under which the hazard takes place. For example, the severity of potential harm to people mingling with moving vehicles will depend on whether this takes place on a busy main road with fast moving traffic or on a quiet side road where the vehicles move slowly.

83 By considering both likelihood and severity for each significant hazard you will be able to judge the size of the remaining risk. Grouping the hazards into high, medium and low risks groups may help you prioritise further actions you need to take to reduce risks.

84 Other tools such as risk classification matrices have been developed, and you may find these helpful if you are organising a complex activity or have large numbers of significant hazards to consider.

Are existing precautions adequate?

85 Some hazards may already be controlled, whether by deliberate measures (eg you may have recently improved the lighting on stairways) or by the circumstances in which they are found (eg street lighting outside the venue may incidentally light the venue entrance stairs). The aim is therefore to identify the precautions and decide whether they are adequate or whether more should be done.

86 Think about how effective the existing precautions are. Look at how they actually work, not how they are supposed to work. Actual practice may differ from what you originally planned. Indeed, this is often where risks creep in unnoticed.

87 Also consider how your precautions may fail or become less effective. For example, features at the venue such as turnstiles could suffer from vandalism, wear and tear, component failure etc. Crowd management arrangements could be hindered by staff confusion over their roles and responsibilities or a breakdown in communication between parties involved in the activity.

88 In order to decide whether the existing precautions are enough, you may wish to make a first rough risk assessment. Consider the risks in the light of existing precautions; trivial risks can usually be ignored as can risks arising from routine activities associated with life in general, unless the activity compounds those risks. In a street event, the pavement kerb could pose a tripping hazard but you could ignore it on the grounds that the risk is no more than that arising from walking along the high street on a normal Saturday

afternoon. If the crowd density is much higher than that on the normal high street, so will be the risk. One reason for this is that people may not see the kerb. Therefore, the previous assessment is no longer valid and this hazard should be evaluated further.

Deciding what more should be done

89 A number of important factors should be considered when deciding what further precautions you need to take to address remaining risks.

90 Have you done all the things that the law says you have to do? For example, the MHSW Regulations require employers, including organisers and contractors, to provide employees with adequate health and safety training and relevant information. Safety signs at the venue must conform to the Health and Safety (Safety Signs and Signals) Regulations 1996.[6]

91 Are generally accepted standards in place? For example, have you taken account of HSE guidance that may relate to your event? This guidance includes publications on fairgrounds,[7] fireworks displays,[8] music events[3] and motor sports.[9]

92 The law also says that you must do what is reasonably practicable to keep your activity safe. 'Reasonably practicable' means that the time, trouble, cost and physical difficulty of taking measures to avoid the risk are not wholly disproportionate to it. The greater the risk, the more likely it is that it is reasonable to go to very substantial expense, trouble and invention to reduce it. But if the consequences and extent of a risk are small, insistence on a great expense would not be considered reasonable. The size or financial position of the employer is not taken into account in this calculation.

Example

The owners of a venue situated adjacent to a busy road identified the high risk of injury to people. There was a high risk of them being struck by a moving vehicle when queuing at the venue entrance. The owners had permanent barriers installed and provided additional stewarding at the entrance to reduce the risk of injury. They regarded this as a 'reasonably practicable' measure to ensure safety. Although the cost of installing the barriers was significant, it was not disproportionate to the high risk of injury.

A further illustration of this point is included in the example of completing a risk assessment at the end of this section.

---

93 The actions you identify should be realistic and give priority to hazards which pose the highest risks. An essential part of your risk assessment is to consider first if it is possible to eradicate the risks altogether. This can usually be achieved by either removing the source of hazard or tackling its causes. For example, it may be possible to exclude all vehicles from the site prior to the event, thus eliminating the risk of people being struck by vehicles during the event.

94 If it is not 'reasonably practicable' to eradicate the risk, then think about how to control the risk (ie to make it less likely to occur or cause harm, to reduce its severity and/or to protect people against harm). For example, the organisers of an open-air festival set aside an area where members of a vintage car club could display their vehicles. To reduce the risk of visitors being struck, the cars had to arrive one hour before the public were admitted and leave one hour after they had left.

95 The section 'Putting precautions in place' covers examples of steps you might take to address risks you have identified.

STEP 4: Record your findings

96 If you have fewer than five employees you are not legally required to write anything down, though it is good practice to keep a written record of what you have done.

However, if you employ five or more people you must record the significant findings of your assessment. Significant findings usually include:

- the significant hazards identified in the assessment;

- the existing precautions in place;

- the remaining risks, including any groups of visitors who are especially at risk; and

- the conclusions of the assessment, including the actions you have identified to further reduce the risks.

97 The law requires you to tell your staff, including any safety representatives, about your findings. The record could be documented in writing by other means (eg electronically), so long as it is available for use by management or for examination (eg by enforcing authority inspectors).

98 Some hazards may have already been dealt with elsewhere. A risk assessment under the Control of Substances Hazardous to Health Regulations 1999 (COSHH)[10] will have addressed the risks associated with the use of hazardous substances. Also, some existing precautions may have already been described in other documents (eg a procedures manual). There is no need to repeat this information in the record - you can simply refer to where it can be found.

STEP 5: Review your assessment and revise it if necessary

99 You are required by law to review your assessment and revise it if there are developments which suggest that your assessment may no longer be valid. Such developments could include:

- major changes to the venue, for example being unable to use waterlogged greenfield parking areas;

- significant changes to the event, for example a last-minute introduction of fairground attractions;

- previous incidents which did or could have injured members of the public; or

- serious incidents at other venues from which you could learn and take preventive action.

Further information about this issue is contained in the 'Review' section.

Completing a risk assessment: an example (family fun day)

STEP 1: Look for the hazards

Crossflow of people near the toilets in the entrance area was identified by the venue owner as a significant hazard.

STEP 2: Decide who might be harmed and how

Staff at the venue had commented that people may cut through other people entering the venue to get to the toilets. This could lead to severe congestion in the venue, pushing and even some minor crushing. A large number of prams and wheelchair-users were anticipated.

STEP 3: Evaluate the risks and decide whether the existing precautions are adequate or whether more should be done

After investigating the crossflow in this busy area, the owner felt it possible that harm could occur (likelihood), resulting in injuries to a number of people who would require first aid (severity). The owner decided that the remaining risk associated with this significant hazard was 'medium'.

Relocation of the toilets was considered in the future, but the costs of doing so were regarded as disproportionate to the improvements that could be achieved to reduce the risks associated with the crossflow. Management decided that this risk reduction method was not 'reasonably practicable'.

The owner decided to reduce the risk by a lower cost option of hiring additional portable toilets for the event and locating them elsewhere. Clear signage and information was provided to reduce the usage of toilets in the entrance area.

STEP 4: Record your findings

Using a risk assessment form, the owner recorded details of the hazard and the people at risk from it. The owner then recorded the risk as 'medium' and wrote down the steps to be taken to address the risk. The employees were told about the new arrangements. When the toilets and signs had been put in place, the owner made a note on the risk assessment form to confirm that the action had been completed.

STEP 5: Review your assessment and revise it if necessary

After the event, the owner and team discussed how effective the arrangements had been, and reviewed the risk assessment. Minor changes to signage were agreed to further reduce risks at such events and the actions recorded on the amended assessment.

Risk assessment - a checklist

It may be helpful to consider the following questions when looking for hazards and completing your risk assessment:

- Are the numbers attending controlled or predictable?

- Are visitors likely to be familiar with the venue?

- Is the event going to attract a particular age group?

- Is the event likely to generate high emotions?

- Is the crowd likely to be mostly male, mostly female or mixed?

- Is the crowd going to be made up of individuals, families or mostly large groups?

- How are you going to cater for particular groups with disabilities?

- How long will the event last?

- How will performers at the event affect the behaviour of the crowd?

- In what ways could media provision at the event affect crowd safety?

- Have you considered possible aggressive behaviour, for example between rival supporters or by visitors towards staff?

- Are gatecrashers likely?

- Will alcohol be available?

- Is it likely that some individuals attending the event have been consuming drugs?

- Are there other major events in the area at the same time as your event?

Putting precautions in place

100 This section provides further details about precautions to address risks to crowd safety that you have identified during your risk assessment. The types of precautions described fall broadly into two categories - the venue and crowd management.

101 The guidance under the following headings illustrates the types of precautions you may need to consider. It does not cover all possible circumstances that may be relevant to your event. References to more detailed guidance are provided.

The venue

102 The following paragraphs cover people's arrival through to their departure. Wherever possible, encourage phased arrivals and departures to prevent overcrowding, for example by:

- making entry cheaper off-peak;

- offering entertainment before and after the main event;

- staggering the start and/or finish of several events within the venue;

- making early arrival and late departure pleasurable by providing good catering and welfare facilities. If possible, provide a place for people who want to eat their own food or just want to sit down.

Transport to and from the venue

103 Ensure that at the planning stage transport facilities (eg bus stops and stations, train stations, car parks) are sufficient to cope with the expected numbers of people. Schedule your event to finish at a time which allows people plenty of time to catch transport.

104 Consider encouraging people to use existing or specially provided public transport systems. For some events you could also consider issuing combination bus or rail tickets.

105 If parking space near the venue is limited or remote sites are used, or it is some distance between the venue and bus/rail stations, consider the use of a shuttle bus service to take people to and from the venue.

Parking

106 Enure that parking arrangements are clearly signposted some distance from the venue, so that the information is conveyed to drivers well in advance.

107 Avoid locating coach drop-off and pick-up points and parking places immediately in front of, or very close to, the entrances/exits to reduce the risk of congestion.

108 Cordon-off areas where parking is potentially dangerous (because it would cause

Combine barriers with effective stewarding

an obstruction, for example to emergency access routes, or an undesirable mix of vehicles and pedestrians) and erect signposts that explain the penalties for illegal parking. It may be necessary to seek the advice of the police about cars that are illegally parked outside the venue.

Access routes to and from the venue

109 Ensure, as far as is possible, that pedestrian routes are separated from vehicle routes. Additional precautions will be required where vehicles form an integral part of the event, for example at motor sport events.

110 Maintain a clear route for emergency vehicles and ensure that the emergency services are aware of the route.

111 Ensure that routes are adequately lit and, where necessary, provide guard rails or barriers to prevent trips or falls.

112 Where possible provide:

- direct routes - to prevent people from trying to take unauthorised short cuts, such as walking on the road among traffic;

- one-way systems - to prevent flows of people in more than one direction;

- separate flows, for example you could set up different pedestrian access routes for visitors arriving from the railway station and those coming from coach/car parks. Separate routes can also be used to reduce conflict between rival supporters;

- routes without pinch points or width changes (slow flows at these points can cause people to become separated). They may wait in other areas to try to rejoin their group, causing further congestion; and

- access routes that are level and ramps for people using wheelchairs.

113 Consider providing facilities such as toilets and refreshments outside the venue for those who arrive early. These can also be used to attract some of the people away from particularly busy routes or areas.

Entrances and exit

114 A combination of barriers and effective stewarding can be used to encourage orderly queuing and movement through entrances and exits. Be careful that queues do not block access or pedestrian flow. Wherever possible, ensure that there is a way by which people can get out of the queue without having to move against the flow or those queuing behind them.

115 Avoid locating ticket sales and pick-up points, temporary structures, attractions, facilities and main information sources close to entrances and exits.

116 Entrances and exits for people with disabilities should be clearly signposted. Provide a separate entrance if large numbers of people are expected; this will avoid disruptions of crowd flows.

117 Don't let people queue on roads, unless there is plenty of room for both people and traffic, and the queue is physically separated by adequate barriers. If this is difficult to achieve, it is better to avoid queuing on roads if possible.

118 Try to avoid letting people queue on stairs, especially if they are used by others, or are part of the means of escape. If it is unavoidable, make certain you have adequate stewards to ensure the queue and adjacent flow of people are well controlled.

119 Try to discourage people from moving forward until doors are fully open. Fix doors in the open position once you have started to let people in or out. If there are other entrances or exits that are not to be used, indicate these types of doors, for example by putting up 'no entry' signs.

120 Take measures at entry points and at sales points to ensure that prohibited items, such as metal cans, glass bottles, or other possible missiles, cannot be taken into the venue. You may find it helpful to use a filter system. For large outdoor events, a system of free flow can help speed up entry to the venue.

Inside the venue

121 Ensure that entrance routes do not filter into vantage points such as popular attractions or front stage areas. This is to avoid people staying at the end of the route and blocking flow into the venue.

122 Crowd surges or pushing should be anticipated when the action in the venue becomes particularly exciting, leading to excess pressure and overcrowding - standing areas are particularly vulnerable. For example:

- the audience may move forward as the main act comes on stage at a music concert; or

- unexpected mass movement of audience members from one attraction or performance to another; or

- in response to cheers and shrieks, the people gathered around an attraction may rush forward to get a better view.

Encourage orderly queuing

123 Protect areas where people are vulnerable to crushing by means of barriers or special design arrangements. For example, relieve and prevent build-up of crowd pressures by using the front of stage barrier used at music events or crush barriers in terraced areas at sports grounds where spectators are standing.

Viewing areas

124 Design viewing areas in such a way that all people have good sight lines to any stage areas. This reduces the tendency of people to crush or surge in order to obtain a better view.

Video or projection screens can be used to attract people away from crowded areas.

125 Ensure that viewing areas are set aside so that people using wheelchairs have a clear view of the attraction and are not affected by crowd movement, such as surging. Be careful that wheelchairs do not block gangways or exits.

Seating areas

126 For seated areas, ensure that the distance between rows of seats is sufficient to enable people to move in and out freely. If temporary seating is provided, it will be necessary to ensure that the seating is adequately secured to avoid 'snaking'.

Fences

127 At outdoor venues, the provision of a fixed boundary will help the safety management of the crowd and prevent trespassers entering the site. For large outdoor events, a substantial perimeter fence may be needed.

Barriers

128 You may need to keep certain areas clear of people, for example an area adjacent to a means of escape. This can be done by barriering-off the areas or obstructing sight lines. For example, side-stage sight lines can be reduced, so that people do not congregate by emergency exits in those areas.

129 Make sure that there are enough facilities (eg refreshments, toilets, welfare and information services, meeting points or waiting areas) provided in the venue to prevent obstruction and congestion through the build-up of queues.

130 The location of facilities, attractions (eg fairground rides) and temporary structures (eg stages, temporary stands, viewing platforms etc) can obstruct entrances, exits or emergency vehicle access and therefore needs to be checked. Ensure that there is sufficient space provided around them for people to move without obstructing flows.

131 You should ensure that adequate inspections and tests are carried out to establish that all structures, installations and equipment, whether permanent or temporary, are safe for the purposes for which they are intended. This is likely to include inspections before, during and after the event. These are equally important for one-day events as for events that last for a number of days.

132 You should ensure that such inspections are carried out by suitably qualified personnel, that a programme of inspections and tests have been drawn up and adhered to, that detailed records of inspections and tests are kept and that adequate resources are allocated to carry out the tasks. Further advice on this can be found in the Institute of Structural Engineers publication *Temporary demountable structures: Guidance on procurement, design and use.*[11]

Crowd management

133 You should provide an adequate number of staff to ensure effective crowd management. Your staffing structure will depend on the size of your event. A large event may require the appointment of a chief steward to be responsible for effective stewarding, supported by a senior supervisor and a number of other supervisors.

134 The staff may also assist the police and other emergency services. Where an event requires the presence of police officers, agree the duties and responsibilities of staff between the organisers and the police.

135 Staff duties include:

- knowing the layout of the site and being able to assist the public by giving information about the available facilities, remembering those with special needs;

- being aware of the location of entrances and exits and first-aid points;

- ensuring that overcrowding does not occur in any part of the venue by managing and directing the crowd, particularly on entering or leaving the venue;

- keeping gangways and exits clear at all times and preventing standing on seats and furniture;

- controlling unruly behaviour and immediately investigating any disturbances or incidents;

- ensuring that combustible litter does not accumulate;

- communicating with supervisors;

- knowing and understanding the arrangements for evacuating the venue, including coded messages and undertaking specific duties in an emergency;

- monitoring of crowds at key points where overcrowding may occur;

- controlling vehicle parking and marshalling traffic.

136 Identify the parts of the venue where staff will be needed and the numbers required to manage the crowd under both normal and emergency situations. Locate staff at key points to manage the crowds. These would include entrances and exits, gangways, barriers, pit areas near the stage at pop concerts etc.

137 Co-ordinate the management of staff from the venue's control point, which needs to maintain an efficient means of communication with the staff and/or their supervisors (see the 'Communication' section).

138 Provide staff with distinctive clothing, such as jackets or tabards which clearly indicate the duty that they are performing (eg steward, traffic marshal supervisor). Provide staff with a means of identification.

139 Train staff to carry out their duties effectively. The type of training will depend on the functions to be performed. Keep a record of the training and instruction provided. Staff with fewer duties (eg controlling parking and marshalling traffic) may not need to cover all elements of the training.

140 Brief staff prior to the event, particularly about communicating with supervisors and others in the event of an emergency. It is recommended that staff receive a written statement of their duties and a plan showing key features of the venue, so that there is less likelihood of information being misinterpreted.

141 Train all supervisory staff in the handling of emergencies, and agree the limits of their responsibilities in conjunction with the emergency services at the planning stage. Inform supervisors of the communications system for the event and the working of the control point (see the 'Communication' section). It is advisable for some of the supervisory staff to have received training in first aid, particularly in cardiac pulmonary resuscitation.

Provide staff with distinctive clothing

142 If you are using a contractor to supply staff, it is recommended that you check that they:

- carry adequate public and employer liability insurance;

- have a company policy on health and safety;

- employ an adequate number of personnel who are competent in the following areas:

  - fire safety and emergency evacuation;

  - basic first aid; and

  - communication procedures.

Where staffing duties are subcontracted (eg to a private stewarding firm), ensure that the contractor's staff meet the required standards.

143 To check that your staffing arrangements are adequate you could, for example:

- check staff training records;

- carry out mock exercises to assess staff training; or

- check procedures are being followed.

Enforcing rules

144 Venue rules (eg those concerning bringing in alcohol, drugs and offensive weapons) need to be enforced firmly and clearly. If appropriate:

- discuss arrangements with the police and think about inviting a special police presence;

- consider introducing some form of penalty for certain types of dangerous behaviour. Penalties could include exclusion from the venue and/or banning from future events;

- publicise the consequences of dangerous behaviour in terms of possible outcome (accidents, injuries, structural collapse etc).

Checking your precautions

145 Check and inspect the precautions you have put in place to ensure they remain effective. Are the arrangements as you planned them? You need to check that stands, attractions etc are sited as planned. Carry out inspections regularly, both before and after members of the public are admitted to the event. Ensure that the persons performing the checks and inspections are competent. Remember to allow enough time for the problems that are discovered to be put right, or for you to find another effective precaution.

146 During the event ensure that all routes, including emergency routes, are kept clear and well signposted. Ensure that arrangements are in place to prevent litter and waste accumulating or being stored in circulation, exit or escape routes.

147 Ensure that any necessary remedial action is taken before the next event. You may find it helpful to write down areas of concern and record when they have been corrected.

When things go wrong

148 Disruptions could happen, for example through:

- equipment failure, eg public address system not working;

- overcrowding, eg through late arrival of large number of people; or

- crowd behaviour, eg surging and pushing, people leaving the venue early, people re-entering the venue.

149 As part of your risk assessment, identify potential disruptions and set up procedures to deal with them (often referred to as 'contingency procedures or plans'). For each disruption, consider the extra resources you will require in staff and equipment (eg loud hailers, additional barrier sections etc). Staff have a key role to play in dealing with disruptions and it is important that they have received adequate training and briefing.

150 Ensure that procedures are made familiar to all relevant staff. Staff meetings or briefings could be used to remind staff about the procedures prior to the staging of the event. Mock exercises are a useful way of testing out your procedures for dealing with disruptions and emergencies.

151 At large events, barriered-off areas, often referred to as 'safety zones', can be designated. If overcrowding threatens, people can be filtered into and through the 'safety zone' to prevent crushing. The use of safety zones needs careful consideration; their possible use should be discussed at the planning stage with relevant parties including the local authorities, the police and emergency services.

152 Planning for emergencies is covered in the 'Emergency planning and procedures' section.

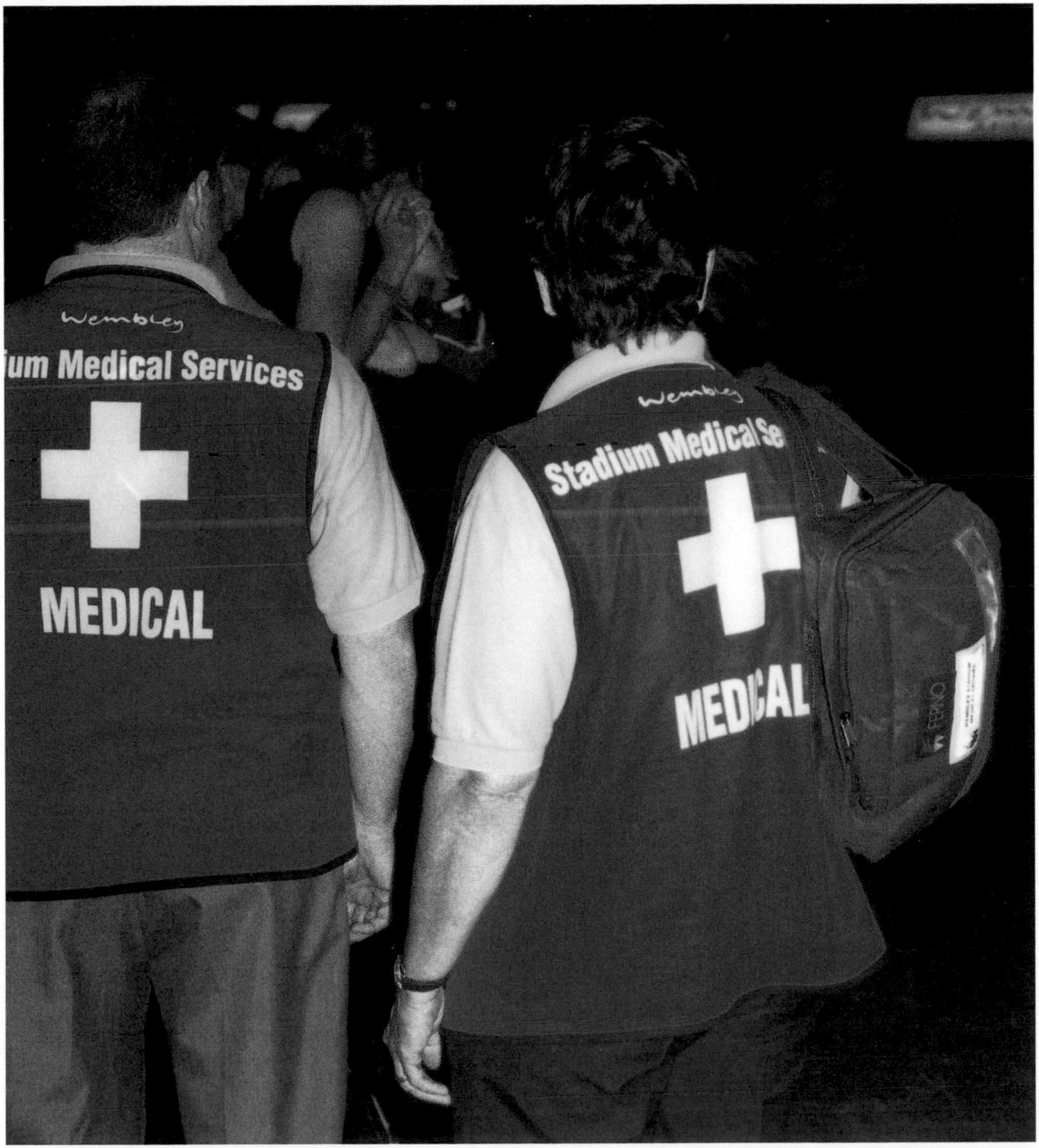
Wembley
ium Medical Services
MEDICAL
Wembley
Stadium Medical Se
MEDICAL

Crowd safety management - a checklist

Communication

- Is the information you will provide to visitors adequate?

- Is the information you will provide to employees and others involved in the event, including emergency services, adequate?

- Have you established clear lines of communication with visitors and others involved with the event?

- Who are the visitors and what do they already know about the venue and the event?

- How could the layout of the venue affect safety and what assistance could you provide for people to find their way about?

- What directions, advice warning or other general information will people need?

- Where, and at what stage of the visit, will people need the information or assistance?

- In what form should the information be presented?

Putting precautions in place

- Are staffing levels, including those for stewards, adequate?

- Are staff competent and adequately trained?

- Are arrangements in place to enforce venue rules, for example those regarding prohibiting the bringing in of alcohol, drugs and offensive weapons?

Monitoring crowds

- Are arrangements in place to monitor the event and detect and deal with any potential problems at an earlier stage?

- Are there sufficient staff to be able to monitor reliably all areas where there are potential crowding problems?

- Are there suitable vantage points available to enable staff on location to monitor all areas effectively?

- Can information collected in a local area of the venue be relayed in an accurate and reliable manner to a central location or control point for control and co-ordination purposes?

- How quickly could crowding develop to a dangerous level at various identified locations?

- How much time is required to respond to crowding problems?

- If a crowding incident occurred, how would you get to know about it so that you could deal with the incident itself and prevent its escalation or reoccurrence?

- Are there enough staff to be able to monitor reliably all areas where there are potential crowding problems?

- Are there enough good vantage points for staff to monitor all areas effectively?

- Can information collected from different areas of the venue be communicated quickly to the control point?

- Can staff at the control point quickly alert staff to a potential problem?

Presence of hazardous items and substances

- Have structures, such as temporary stands, been inspected by a competent person to ensure against collapse?

- Has the position of structures been checked prior to the activity to ensure that they do not restrict access routes?

- Are any fireworks to be used stored safely and are adequate procedures in place for their safe use?

- Are adequate precautions in place to prevent visitors from being struck by vehicles in and around the area of the event?

- Has the effect on crowd safety of any special effects (eg lasers, dry ice etc) been adequately addressed?

- Has equipment installed to ensure effective crowd movement (eg escalators, turnstiles, ticket machines etc) been adequately maintained?

- Are the risks associated with substances hazardous to health (eg fumes form generators) adequately controlled?

- Are potentially hazardous areas, such as plant rooms, switchgear and chemical storage areas, inaccessible to unauthorised persons?

- Have sources of fire been adequately dealt with, for example hot food stalls, LPG cylinders on stalls and in caravans, petrol generators, smoking, lighting of fires by visitors etc?

Emergency planning and procedures

What is a crowd safety emergency?

153 The term 'emergency' is taken to mean a situation where the emergency services become actively involved or an urgent evacuation is required. Broadly, they will be situations with the potential for serious injuries requiring immediate and specialist action beyond the capabilities of venue staff.

154 Emergencies may include fire or explosions, bomb threats, collapse of a structure (eg seating, staging, fairground attraction), release of hazardous substances (eg gas leak), or unanticipated, hostile weather conditions (eg flooding, high winds).

155 The significance of crowd management for emergency planning is that crowd disorder and overcrowding can be factors in the creation of emergencies (eg overloading of barriers, staging etc, behavioural problems such as violence or panic) and are also factors which make dealing with emergencies more difficult if they do occur.

Measures to manage emergency situations

156 The types of measures you put in place will depend on the findings of your risk assessment. They will also be influenced by your consultations with other relevant parties including:

- authorities who enforce the relevant legislation, eg local authority, fire authority and any relevant government departments;

- emergency services, including the police, nearby hospitals and on-site first-aid providers;

- all those involved in the operation, such as the venue owner, security firms and vendors operating at the venue;

- nearby sites and transport operators, which could be affected by the emergency or subsequent evacuation.

Any discussions need to include the consideration of the safety of the emergency services, as well as that of the public, your own staff and others on-site.

157 This section sets out key issues that should be covered in emergency procedures to minimise risks due to crowding during emergency situations. It does not attempt to provide guidance on the general subject of dealing with emergencies; further information is available on this from other sources.

158 It is important to keep written emergency procedures together as an emergency plan. Ensure that copies of emergency procedures or plans are easily accessible to managers, supervisors, stewards, other relevant staff and personnel from outside bodies (eg local authority contractors, vendors, emergency services). Cover the procedures in training and reinforce during event briefings; this will help staff to act confidently and efficiently during an emergency. Basic procedures and other relevant information could be put on a small card or sheet provided to all staff. Consider carrying out mock exercises to ensure that your procedures will be effective in the event of an emergency. Emergency procedures should cover the areas dealt with in the following paragraphs.

Informing the emergency services

159 Decide who will contact the emergency services in the event of an emergency and who will deputise in their absence. They should be clear on their responsibilities.

160 Once an emergency is identified (in the case of bomb threat, when a suspicious package is discovered or a warning telephone call received), the police and other relevant emergency services, including those responsible for 'accident investigation', need to be told as soon as possible. It may be helpful if checklists of information obtained are passed to relevant staff, or at key locations such as the control point. The obtained information could include:

- the exact official address of the venue;

- the nature of the emergency, accident or incident and its extent, if known;

- the access route and meeting point. The previously agreed access may no longer be suitable due to the circumstances of the emergency;

- any relevant information about hazards, eg storage of chemicals;

- make sure that there is a system for passing on information to all venue staff and any relevant outside bodies. Clearly specify who should be informed and in what order.

161 Further guidance for managers and security officers on bomb incidents and threats is contained in the Home Office handbook *Bombs: Protecting people and property*.[12]

Communicating with staff

162 Different levels of urgent response may be necessary, from injury or sickness of one person to a major incident that requires urgent evacuation. It is therefore important that a competent person(s) with authority to stop the

Are communication systems adequate?

flows. You could do this by two-way radio, or by coded public address messages. The latter can also be used to signal to staff to listen to radio messages or to contact the control point through the internal telephone system.

164 You need to decide what to tell staff. Information could include: the nature of the emergency, the location and the affected areas, the procedures to follow, and any special information about which escape routes or exits should not be used.

Communicating with the public within the vicinity of the event

165 You will need to consider what to tell the public about the emergency, and when. Whether the whole venue is told at once will depend on the nature of the emergency.

166 People may be confused and unsure of what action to take in an unfamiliar situation. Some may be more concerned about making alternative arrangements, such as looking for separated friends/family or telephoning home about a delay. The way you provide instructions can address these concerns and influence the speed of the public response.

167 It will help to give short, clear instructions, repeat important information and phrase instructions positively (eg 'Use the green door', not 'Do not use the red door').

event is designated at the planning stage. Since each link in a communication chain is a potential source of misunderstanding, breakdown or delay, alerting chains should be as short as possible.

163 Make sure that there is a system for passing on information to all venue staff and any relevant outside bodies. Clearly specify who should be informed and in what order. Staff need to be kept informed about any emergencies within the venue in a way that does not alert the crowd before staff are ready and in a position to handle the sudden

Be polite, firm and calm. It is important to ensure that the information is presented in a way that is not alarming.

168 People can be informed about evacuation by combinations of the following means:

- recorded or live PA messages;

- word of mouth by staff (including the use of loud hailers);

- audible alarms;

- information boards (including scoreboards, star screen etc).

169 Information to be given to the public might include:

- which exits to use and how to get there;

- where to assemble, if appropriate;

- the reason for the instructions (eg 'to avoid overcrowding in Area A, please use...');

- an assurance to people that arrangements will be made to compensate them or to refund/reschedule the event;

- telling people where the meeting point(s) are for friends/relatives who have got separated;

- availability of toilets and telephones outside the venue; and

- providing information on any transport arrangements that are available.

Evacuation

170 People tend to evacuate via the routes and exits with which they are most familiar. Unless clear directions are given, this could result in overloading of certain routes and exits. You will need to ensure arrangements are made to make use of all available exits, and people are directed to the most appropriate escape route and exit. It may be necessary to redeploy staff to help in the most crowded areas.

171 Ensure suitable arrangements are made to provide assistance to people with special needs, adults with young children and pushchairs etc during the evacuation. Such assistance will help these people and also reduce the likelihood of both crushing and overcrowding. You may also need to set up barriers and signs and help staff and police turn away those arriving at the venue as quickly as possible.

172 If the layout of the venue is complex, or the size of the area to be evacuated is particularly large or distant from the exits, it may be more practical to ask people to gather at various safe points in the venue and then escort them in groups to the exits.

173 Staff need clear guidance on what to do if someone refuses to co-operate, for example going in the wrong direction or being reluctant to leave. Staff should try to find out what the problem is if time permits. The person(s) may have a problem that can easily be solved, or know of a problem which you don't, such as a blocked exit. If their refusal to follow instructions is likely to endanger the safety of others, staff should seek help from a supervisor or event promoter or manager. If danger is involved, don't waste time on it - turn to more urgent tasks.

174 Maintain a clear route for emergency vehicles and ensure that the emergency services are aware of the route. This is to avoid emergency vehicles having to compete with departing or other traffic or the evacuating crowds in order to get to the venue.

Consider phasing departure

Assembly areas

175 Safe assembly areas are vital for successful evacuation. Ensure there are enough assembly areas and that they are big enough to accommodate the crowd. Situate these areas away from vulnerable areas such as flammable or chemical stores or car parks in bomb threat situations. Ensure that signs are prominent and that the location of assembly areas on venue maps or programmes is clearly marked. This will make it easier to direct the crowd to them when an evacuation is necessary.

176 Provide people in assembly areas with:

- relevant information (eg closure of car parks, availability of facilities such as toilets, telephones and meeting points etc); and

- updated information on what is happening at regular intervals (eg whether and when the venue is likely to be reopened, or if the event is likely to continue etc).

177 The information could be provided via your public address system or by staff using loud hailers. This assists other staff to carry out their tasks without frequent interruption from members of the public seeking information.

178 If departure en masse as a result of an emergency or otherwise is likely to lead to congestion of departure routes or hamper emergency services, ensure there are sufficient stewards to control a phased departure.

Reopening the venue

179 You will need to consider the implications of reopening the venue once it is safe to do so - issues include:

- whether you can readmit the people safely in a short time;

- anticipated crowd reaction to closure or reopening;

- whether there will be transport to take people home after the planned closing time; and

- refund arrangements.

180 Set up procedures to manage the reopening of the venue. These procedures would ensure an orderly reoccupation and avoid overcrowding due to the heavy and sudden flows created by people who may be in a hurry to get back into the venue. Ensure staff are in position before allowing people to re-enter the venue. Position staff at the likely 'pinch points' in order to form orderly flows or queues.

Things that can go wrong - a checklist

Have all foreseeable scenarios that could disrupt the event been considered? For example:

- Have you consulted relevant parties, eg local authority, police, fire authority, emergency services, transport operators, about planning for possible emergencies?

- Have you considered possible disruptions and emergencies in your risk assessment?

- Do you have procedures in place to deal with possible disruptions and emergencies?

- Do employees and other staff understand the procedures?

- Are the procedures covered in training and reinforced during event briefings?

- Have you carried out mock exercise(s) to check that your procedures work?

Communication

59

181 Good communication is an essential feature of managing crowd safety. Organisers, their staff and other personnel all have a key role to play.

Communication with the public

182 If you fail to provide the right information at an early enough stage, visitors may quickly become confused. For example, they may stop or slow down to search for information, or suddenly change direction, being unsure about where to go. This could lead to overcrowding or obstruction of flows.

183 People experiencing difficulties in obtaining information may feel unsatisfied, discontented or even become aggressive. They may be less likely to comply with instructions.

184 There are many ways of communicating effectively with the public; examples are shown in Table 1 on page 62. Whatever methods you decide to use, ensure that your communication system provides accurate, up-to-date and relevant information, for example when certain tickets are sold out or an attraction is temporarily closed. Consider relaying information in languages other than English if necessary, for example if there is likely to be a proportionately large number of people from an ethnic group.

185 Communications play an essential role in managing the flow of people, for example by encouraging people to use alternative or under-used routes, entrances and exits. Selective information can be given to people coming from different directions to direct them to certain routes and entrances and exits.

186 Wherever possible, ensure that information is given to the public in advance to help them plan. For example:

- transport details, meeting points, venue rules and prohibitions could be printed on the ticket or promotional leaflet;

- display boards at the venue's entrance(s)/exit(s) could be used to inform people about items such as tickets that they need to have ready or prohibited items that cannot be brought into the event. This may reduce congestion at ticket checkpoints; or

Example: Event in park

People familiar with a park are likely to follow park paths rather than those set out for the event, even if this means cutting through crowds. Routes would therefore need to be considered in planning. Good signage and effective stewarding would be essential.

Provide clear announcements

- a formal press release, letter drop, or advertisements could be used to provide information to the local community.

187 Inform people promptly when an event is postponed or transport is delayed; this could be done via display boards, public address system or loud hailers. Inform people of the measures that are in place to deal with the changes. Remember that for evening events people may arrive in the light and leave in darkness - they could be disorientated.

188 Ensure that all signs, and particularly those relating to fire safety and emergency evacuation, are presented and sited so that, as far as is possible, they can be easily seen by people with impaired vision or colour perception. Clear, audible public address announcements are vital for safety of people with impaired vision. People with impaired hearing rely on the presentation of clear, informative visual information.

Communication between staff

189 Crowding incidents can develop very quickly; good communications enable you to make a rapid and organised response.

Control point

190 You need to ensure the flow of essential information between all staff concerned with crowd management, during normal operations and in emergencies. The use of a central location or control point to co-ordinate the flow of information can assist you to:

- gain an overall picture at the venue, eg size of crowd, build-up of queues, serious incidents;

- co-ordinate the response of all staff responsible for crowd management; and

- co-ordinate actions with other departments, emergency services or other external bodies.

191 For small venues, the control point can be in the form of a manager's office with basic communication equipment (eg telephone and a two-way radio) and necessary plans and procedures. At an outside event, it could be a tent or cabin. For a street event, you may need to choose a 'primary site' (eg beginning or end of carnival route to base the control point).

Table 1 Ways to communicate with the public

Method of communication	Comments
Tickets, leaflets, posters and promotional material	Can provide information about transport and venue entry details and layout, house rules and prohibitions. Leaflets for residents in parade areas - parking, recommending carrying ID etc.
Signs	Need to be sufficiently large, clear, legible and suitably positioned. They include safety signs (eg 'no smoking', 'emergency escape' etc) and information signs (eg directional signs, venue plans, venue rules).
Noticeboards and electronic information display boards	Can display essential information such as prohibition on cans and bottles being taken into the venue or no-smoking. Information on changes such as transport delays, opening of alternative entrances or emergency information can easily be displayed.
Public address systems	The system should be audible, clear and intelligible. It can be used to inform, advise and direct people. The system can help to free staff from answering questions regarding delays or changes, so that they can carry on with their duties. The individual making the announcements should have a calming voice.
Communication to individuals by staff	A helpful way of giving specific advice, directions and instructions to individuals or small groups during normal and emergency situations. The information should be clearly given and accurate.
Information desks	Can provide specific advice, directions and answer specific enquiries.
National or local radio and press	Can provide details of transport (eg routes to take), any changes to the event or venue or late information such as forecast of bad weather that will affect an outdoor event.

192 A major venue, on the other hand, may require a purpose-built central control room equipped with closed circuit TV monitors etc. Control rooms are particularly useful in emergency situations, where the actions of venue staff and emergency services need to be closely co-ordinated.

193 If you need frequent communications with outside bodies or others, such as a stewarding company assisting with your event, think about sharing a central control point with them, positioning your central control point near to theirs, or setting up a permanent communications link between the control points.

194 Bear in mind the following points when considering where to locate control points and how to equip them.

- Try to avoid locating near any potential hazards or high-risk areas.

- Access should be controlled, and entrance restricted to authorised personnel only.

- If several items of electrical equipment are installed, an appropriate fire extinguisher should be provided.

- Try to reduce the glare on closed circuit TVs or visual display unit screens from natural and artificial lighting.

- General noise levels should be kept to a minimum, so that staff can communicate without difficulty.

- Try to keep all appropriate equipment within easy reach of everyone who needs to use it.

- Consider installing emergency back-up power supplies, emergency lighting and back-up monitoring and communication systems.

- Consider identifying a secondary control point in case an emergency should require one.

Ways of communicating

195 Many ways of communicating are available for use in public venues, ranging from simple verbal messages to radio and telephone systems. Examples are shown in Table 2 at the end of this section. Choose systems appropriate for your venue that are effective, clear, and reliable. Organise routine checks and tests of your communication systems.

196 During an event monitor the systems, including simple verbal ones, to ensure that they are working effectively. For example, the venue manager could be provided with a portable radio which is left switched on while they are on duty.

197 The failure of electrical communications systems needs to be considered. Provision could include:

■ spare mobile phones or radios;

■ back-up loud hailers in the event of failure of the public address system; and

■ at larger venues, back-up power supply for the public address system.

198 Further information on communication systems is contained in the *Guide to safety at sports grounds.*

Communication procedures

199 Establish clear procedures that define what needs to be communicated to whom, by whom and when. Think about developing standard procedures for communications between staff. For example, a radio communication might consist of the following:

■ who is calling;

■ where they are calling from;

■ the message itself; and

■ confirmation of the message.

200 Ensure that no confusion can arise about areas of the venue being discussed in communications. Areas of the venue could be given agreed names or numbers etc that are clearly understood by all staff. A grid map is often used for large outdoor events to assist staff to identify a location at the venue. To ensure that communication tasks are properly carried out, consider providing checklists for the staff concerned. A checklist for an emergency might indicate who should be contacted and in which order.

201 Think about keeping some forms of communication for high-priority use only, such as a radio channel solely for the use of the medical or health and safety teams.

202 At an event where many people are involved, such as a street parade, consider requesting that standard messages are used between stewards and to the public so as to avoid inconsistent information and approach.

Communication with outside bodies

203 Decide who is responsible for key co-ordination tasks in emergency or other contingency situations, In particular, decide who speaks to emergency services, other local venues, transport organisations and other outside bodies. If you need to have special transport arrangements, maintain communications channels with transport authorities, the police and motoring organisations throughout the planning period and during the event itself, making contingency plans to deal with the results of traffic conditions.

Table 2 Communicating in public venues

Way of communicating	How it is used
Briefings/debriefings - Reviews	To provide information about crowd safety issues and emergency procedures prior to the opening of the venue. For collecting observations and feedback comments after the event or following an evacuation.
Verbal commands/hand signals	Where staff are working in visual contact or in close proximity to a noisy area.
Public address system	Apart from its use in communicating with the public, it also allows staff to respond to broadcast public information messages, or to coded messages alerting them to respond to a problem.
Telephone	Where staff are based at fixed locations (eg turnstiles) or for emergency communications from key locations (eg next to emergency exits) and where staff report in at intervals.
Radio system/portable phones	Where staff operate over a wide area, there is a need for close co-ordination and/or a fast communication with other colleagues or supervisory staff.

204 Traffic conditions may affect the timing of people's arrival or departure plans. Keep in close contact with the police or motoring organisations for updated traffic reports.

205 Ensure that good communication links (eg direct phone lines) are maintained with bus, tube and rail stations close to the venue. If, for example, a train is delayed, this information can be relayed to visitors. If your event is likely to affect traffic to and from nearby events or venues, ensure the organisers are informed.

Monitoring crowds

206 The monitoring of crowd behaviour is a key component of crowd management, enabling you to detect crowding problems at an early stage. You can also assess how effective your crowd safety precautions are.

207 Effective monitoring can help avoid overcrowding problems and aid long-term action to correct problems in venue design or event management. Three key areas to consider are:

- overall number of people (to ensure that the overall venue capacity is not likely to be exceeded);

- distribution of people (to help prevent local overcrowding); and

- identifying potential crowd problems (to prevent problems such as public disorder from escalating and leading to overcrowding).

Where to monitor

208 As part of your risk assessment, identify potential problem areas which will need to be closely monitored. Such areas may include:

CCTV can be a helpful addition

- entrances and exits;

- standing areas with a potential for crowd surges or pushing;

- popular stalls, attractions, exhibits and refreshments;

- bottlenecks (eg stairs, escalators etc);

- areas where people queue; and

- enclosed or confined areas.

How to monitor

Counting systems

209 Counting systems can help you estimate the number of people within your venue or area of the venue. Design these systems to provide information to staff at the control point as to how quickly people are entering and when and if an area is expected to become full.

210 Examples of counting systems include:

- hand counters. These can be used at entrances to avoid double counting;

- providing wristbands to allow people to enter particular areas such as a standing area at a music event. Overcrowding can be prevented by only issuing an agreed set number of wristbands;

- turnstiles linked to automatic counting systems; and

- computerised systems linked to sensors at entry points.

211 The following ways of counting may be more appropriate to venues where there are few defined boundaries, such as street events or stations and shopping malls where people are continuously arriving and leaving throughout the day:

- sampling flow rates at entrances to estimate numbers entering or leaving the venue;

- monitoring of cars and coaches entering the venue and checking how full the parking areas are;

- using closed circuit television (CCTV) or staff at vantage points to view the crowd and estimate numbers; and

- estimating the number of people based on advanced bookings, transportation schedules or previous experience.

Staff within the crowd

212 This enables staff to experience crowding conditions at first hand. It also enables them to observe people's faces, identify signs of distress and sense atmospheres or tension. Staff on hand can help to assist people or to diffuse any dangerous behaviour such as jumping onto seats or 'surfing' the crowd. Staff may discourage dangerous behaviour by their presence in the crowd.

213 Where monitoring is done by staff stationed at particular posts, ensure that they occupy vantage points where they can scan a sufficiently large area and their lines of sight are not obstructed.

214 Monitoring can also be carried out by staff patrolling the venue. This is appropriate

Patrolling the venue

where crowding problems are likely to develop slowly at particular points within the venue. Staff may be given specific areas to check at regular intervals.

215 If monitoring is done by staff at the same time as other duties, such as ticket checking, ensure they have sufficient opportunities to monitor the crowd. Otherwise, consider having additional staff to reduce their workload or to monitor and control crowds during busy periods.

Closed circuit television (CCTV)

216 CCTV systems can vary from a few fixed cameras at key locations through to extensive coverage using a large number of remote operation cameras with zoom lens. CCTV allows an overview of sections such as entrances, departure routes and problem areas relayed directly to the control point.

217 The systems can provide information on distribution in a number of areas and are useful for directing and monitoring crowd management operations. CCTV is particularly useful to monitor areas which would otherwise require a great deal of staffing. A CCTV system should never be considered as a substitute for good stewarding or other forms of safety management. It should be viewed as a helpful addition.

218 Ensure that the CCTV system is adequately maintained and inspected. Develop a contingency plan to cover power supply or system failure. For large events, an auxiliary power supply may be appropriate. Further guidance on CCTV systems can be found in the *Guide to safety at sports grounds*.

219 You may find it appropriate to use a selection of the systems described to effectively monitor your event. For example, you could use CCTV at fixed locations, supported by staff watching the crowd from vantage points, while others patrol the venue.

Estimating the crowd

220 When monitoring the size of the crowd, the following are useful indicators:

- space between people;

- rough count of people in a small identifiable area (eg between four columns) which can be scaled up; and

- rate of flow into or out of an area (ie the number of people or size of crowd passing a marked object).

221 When monitoring changes in the behaviour of the crowd, the following are useful indicators:

- signs of distress;

- pushing and surging; and

- shouting or similar indications of bad temper or excitement.

Review

222 Review your activity and consider all aspects of the arrangements you have put in place to manage crowd safety. The review can be in the light of a recent event (eg football match, street festival) or a period of operation of a venue (eg conference centre, shopping mall, railway station).

223 Reviews are vitally important to ensure that your crowd safety arrangements are relevant to and appropriate for your next event or to the changing needs of your venue and its visitors. Your review will help to identify areas where changes are needed and/or introduce suggested improvements. It may be helpful to use the section headings in this publication as a guide to ensure that you cover all the key issues during your review.

Aims

224 You should aim to:

- involve staff in the review and encourage them to discuss concerns;

- identify and cater for any changes to the venue, eg staffing structure, type of people attending the venue, temporary changes due to building work;

- identify the causes of any particular problems or accidents that occurred at the event or during venue operation. Include incidents that possibly could

have led to injury or damage ('near misses');

- identify ways of improving the management of crowd safety; and

- collect feedback from those involved in the event or operation of the venue.

225 The conclusions or key points, successes and failures from the review process need to be fed back to all those involved in the event. This is a useful way to motivate staff to improve performance.

Timing

226 Review your event as soon as possible after it has finished, in order to ensure that any problems are still relatively fresh in people's memories.

227 If many of the staff are likely to disperse, you may wish to carry out a rapid debriefing as soon as practicable and use the report of this in the full review. Some event managers carry out a debriefing immediately after the event. They then look at the issues raised before their next event and modify plans and procedures in the light of those issues.

228 Whatever approach you adopt, agree the nature and timing of the review before the event starts. Arrangements for addressing

Review event safety as soon as possible

Involve staff in the review

issues raised in the review can also be agreed at this stage. For venues used on a routine basis (eg shopping malls), reviews could be carried out regularly (ie monthly, annually) and certainly after any major problems or incidents or when any changes in venue design or procedures are considered.

Who to involve

229 In general, representatives of all parties involved in the event should take part in the review. Where possible, select representatives who can give you the fullest picture of all aspects of the event.

230 Specific training for your own staff involved in the review process can help to improve its effectiveness. If there are a large number of people involved, you may find it more manageable to have a number of separate reviews examining particular issues, which can then be combined.

What information to collect

231 The process of review is based on information gathered during an event or the running of a venue. You can gather this information in a number of ways, some are suggested below. The way you collect information should also be periodically reviewed and updated.

Sources of information

232 You could consider the following sources of information:

- debriefing meeting after events - for events run over several days, collect comments made at staff meetings and updates during the event;

- think about setting up a reporting system to record the concerns of individual members of staff and members of the public;

- using a reporting system which documents incidents, near misses, good and bad features of operations etc; and

- health and safety inspections by your own staff or enforcing authority inspectors.

Types of information

233 It is important to consider:

- the effectiveness of your plans, risk assessments and procedures, for example how well a new procedure worked for improving supervisors' responses to information from stewards or whether the new type of barrier was effective; and

- indications of problems, for example areas of crowd build-up, sudden crowd movements, complaints by members of the public. In each instance, it is very important to try to identify both the obvious and underlying causes of the problem.

After your review

234 Based on the information you have collected, your review will help you to decide if your arrangements for managing crowd safety are adequate. It may be necessary to take remedial action to improve aspects of your arrangements. Risk assessments may need to be modified. It is important to decide who is responsible for taking the action and the time for its completion.

235 To assist in future planning, you should keep a record of the findings of the review. The record is particularly important where there are changes in the personnel responsible for crowd safety.

Appendix:
Relevant legislation

The Health and Safety at Work etc Act 1974

1   The Health and Safety at Work etc Act 1974 (HSW Act) applies to all employers, employees and self-employed people. The Act protects not only people at work but also members of the public and volunteers who may be affected by a work activity. Arranging and running an event counts as work activity.

Duties of employers to employees

2   All employers have a general duty under the Act to make sure that, so far as reasonably practicable, the health, safety and welfare of their employees are protected when they are at work. In practical terms, employers must make sure that:

- the workplace is safe and without risks;

- safe working procedures are set and followed;

- machinery and equipment is properly maintained and safe to use;

- equipment and harmful substances are used properly and stored safely;

- employees are provided with the information, instruction, training and supervision necessary for them to work safely; and

- employees have healthy working conditions, including adequate lighting, heating, ventilation and toilet facilities.

3   Employers with five or more employees must prepare a written health and safety policy. The safety policy must set out the employer's aims and objectives for improving health and safety for their employees. It must also set out the organisation and arrangements in place for achieving those objectives. 'Organisation' can be taken to mean people and their responsibilities, and 'arrangements' to mean systems and procedures.

4   Employers are required to bring the health and safety policy to the notice of all their employees and to keep their policy up to date. Revisions will be necessary if, for example, procedures included in the policy are changed or if the policy names particular individuals as being responsible for aspects of health and safety and there are subsequent changes in personnel.

5   Recognised trade unions have the right to appoint safety representatives on behalf of the employees in consultations with their employer about health and safety matters.

6   Any employees not in groups covered by trade union safety representatives must be consulted by their employers. The employer can choose to consult them directly or through elected representatives.

Duties of employers to people not employed by them

7   Employers and self-employed people have a responsibility for the health and safety of members of the public, other self-employed people or contractors' employees who may be affected by their undertaking.

8   The people who should be considered include the following:

- people attending the event;

- stewards or volunteers; and

- food and merchandise vendors or contractors erecting temporary stands.

9   Contractors and people such as vendors also have their own duties to comply with health and safety legislation. However, they may need to be given information about a site so that they are not put at risk. Those hiring contractors may need to exchange information about the way in which a job is to be carried out, so that their own employees or members of the public are not put in danger.

Duties of employees

10 Under the HSW Act, employees have a legal duty to take reasonable care of themselves and other people and co-operate with their employer where safety is concerned.

Duties of self-employed people

11 Self-employed people have duties under the HSW Act similar to those for employers and should not create risks to themselves or other people. They may also be subject to the requirements of the Regulations made under the HSW Act. Although only the courts can give an authoritative interpretation of law, in considering the application of these Regulations and guidance to people working under another's direction, the following should be considered:

If people working under the control and direction of others are treated as self-employed for tax and national insurance purposes they are nevertheless treated as their employees for health and safety purposes. It may therefore be necessary to take appropriate action to protect them. If any doubt exists about who is responsible for the health and safety of a worker this could be clarified and included in the terms of a contract. However, remember, a legal duty under section 3 of the HSW Act cannot be passed on by means of a contract and there will still be duties towards others under section 3 of the HSW Act. If such workers are employed on the basis that they are responsible for their own health and safety, legal advice should be sought before doing so.

Duties of people in control of premises

12 The HSW Act places duties on anyone who has control to any extent of non-domestic premises (eg public venues) used by people who are not their employees (eg members of public attending an event). These duties overlap to some extent with the duties of employers and the self-employed to people who are not employees.

13 The duties apply to premises where machinery or equipment or substances are provided for use of others. The duties also apply when people enter to work there, for example contractors who go into premises to install or repair machinery.

14 Every person in control of non-domestic premises has a duty to take such steps as are reasonable in their position to ensure, so far as is reasonably practicable, that there are no risks to health and safety. The duty extends to the non-domestic premises themselves, any connected non-domestic premises such as corridors, staircases or storage spaces, the ways into and out of non-domestic premises, and any machinery or materials in the non-domestic premises.

15 The duty applies to persons such as owners and occupiers of non-domestic premises, or persons who by virtue of a contract or tenancy agreement have specific obligations in respect of the repair or maintenance of premises or to ensure that machinery or substances are safe and without risks to health.

The Management of Health and Safety at Work Regulations 1999

16 The Management of Health and Safety at Work Regulations 1999 (the MHSW Regulations) require employers and the self-employed to assess the risks to employees and non-employees (eg members of the public) arising from work activities. This is in order to identify the control measures which need to be taken to comply with relevant health and safety legislation, eliminating risks where possible and reducing risk from those activities which remain.

17 Where there are five or more employees, the significant findings of the assessment must be recorded. These should include:

- a record of the preventive and protective measures in place to control the risks;

- what further action, if any, needs to be taken to reduce risk sufficiently; and

- demonstrable proof that a suitable and sufficient assessment has been made.

An assessment should be reviewed if there are developments that suggest that it may no longer be valid (or that it can be improved). The assessment should, if necessary, be modified.

18 Employers are required to have arrangements for effective planning, organisation, control, monitoring and review of preventive and protective measures (ie health and safety precautions). The MHSW Regulations cover key aspects of health and safety arrangements for ensuring the safety of crowds. Further general guidance can be found in the HSE publication *Managing health and safety: Five steps to success*.[13]

19 The Regulations require employers to appoint a competent person to assist them with their health and safety duties. Employers should look to appoint competent person(s), where they exist, from among their employees in preference to external sources of competent advice and assistance. External sources of competent advice and assistance should be sought if no internal source exists or it is insufficient to provide employers with the help they need.

20 Employers are required to provide employees with adequate health and safety training and comprehensible and relevant information.

21 The Regulations also require that temporary workers (ie those who are employed under a fixed-term contract of employment) must be given certain information about health and safety information before their duties begin.

22 Where employers share their workplace with another employer or self-employed person, or have another employer's staff working in their premises, they have a duty to co-operate with each other, take all reasonable steps to co-ordinate measures taken by them to comply with the Fire Precautions (Workplace) Regulations 1997,[14] and exchange information on health and safety. Every employer and self-employed person must ensure that employees of any other employer working in their workplace are provided with comprehensible information on risks to their health and safety arising from the work activity and control measures introduced to comply with the law.

23 The Regulations also require employers to arrange necessary contacts with the emergency services with regard to first aid, emergency medical care and rescue work, as well as requiring them to have procedures in place to deal with serious and imminent danger. This might include evacuation of the workplace. The employer must nominate a sufficient number of people to implement the procedures. They should be trained and competent to carry out their role in an emergency situation.

The Health and Safety (First-Aid) Regulations 1981

24 Under the Regulations, arrangements for first aid should be made at places where people work. The level of first aid needed depends on a number of factors, including the number of employees and the type of work

- recording the details on a computer; or

- maintaining a written log.

Fire safety legislation

32 The Fire Precautions (Workplace) Regulations 1997, as amended, came into effect on 1 December 1999. They removed virtually all exceptions from the regulations, particularly premises with fire certificates. Your responsibility extends beyond compliance with the requirements of the regulations in relation to matters within the employer's control. You must:

- carry out a fire risk assessment of the site of the event. All employees and those who attend who may be affected by a fire, including those with special needs, must be taken into account - record the findings of your risk assessment if you employ more than five people;

- provide and maintain adequate fire precautions and safeguard occupants of the site by such means as properly maintained fire-fighting equipment and fire detectors, emergency routes and exits; and

- provide information and instruction to your employees about what to do in an emergency.

33 You have six further legal duties:

- you must nominate employees, possibly yourself, to undertake special roles identified in your emergency plan;

- you must consult your employees, or their representatives, about these nominations and about proposals to improve fire precautions;

- you must inform other employers who share the location of potentially major risks that might affect the safety of their employees - you must also co-operate with them regarding measures proposed to reduce or control those risks;

- if you are not an employer, but control a location that accommodates several events, you must ensure compliance with the fire regulations in those areas that you control;

- your employees must co-operate to ensure the site is safe from fire and avoid placing themselves or other people at risk; and

- you must establish a suitable means of contacting the emergency services, and ensure that they can be called easily.

34 The Fire Precautions Act 1971[22] works primarily through fire certification procedures. If you are in any doubt about whether you need

to obtain a fire certificate for your event or at your venue, you should seek advice from your local fire authority. Specifications for means of escape in new, extended or altered premises are contained in the relevant Building Regulations.

35 Musical events are subject to the requirements of the Fire Precautions (Workplace) Regulations 1997, as amended, and the Fire Precautions Act 1971. The regulations also apply to any tent or moveable structure. Further guidance includes the *Guide to fire precautions in existing places of entertainment and like premises.*[23]

36 The MHSW Regulations require you to assess the risks to employees and those who attend an event, so that you can decide what measures are necessary to comply with health and safety law. This includes protection from fire, an assessment of its likelihood and consequences, and the need for measures to reduce or eliminate such risks.

37 *Fire safety: An employer's guide*[24] contains guidelines on how to draw up an emergency plan and deals with general fire precautions.

38 If you are in doubt about any aspect of fire safety, you should consult your local fire authority.

Sports grounds

39 Fire precautions in sports grounds with a local authority safety certificate, issued under the Safety of Sports Grounds Act 1975[25] or the Fire Safety and Safety of Places of Sport Act 1987,[26] form a single element of integrated requirements for spectators' safety. Different authorities should enforce conflicting requirements. The fire authority should consult the local authority issuing the safety certificate.

40 Local authorities issue, monitor or enforce safety certificates for sports grounds. They can set or reduce capacities or issue prohibition notices under sports grounds legislation. However, with fire precautions based on your risk assessment under the Fire Regulations, a safety certificate that contravenes the Fire Regulations may be revoked. Local authorities have legal power to amend safety certificates.

Entertainment which requires a licence

41 Several forms of entertainment require a licence from the local authority or licensing magistrate. These licences can impose additional fire safety requirements and standards of safety and hygiene, which may go beyond the minimum levels needed by the Fire Regulations. The most common events which are subject to licensing control involve:

- the sale of alcohol;

- music and dancing;

- theatrical performances;

- the showing of films;

- gambling;

- sporting activities; and

- other forms of public entertainment.

42 Permanent venues usually have an annual entertainment licence granted with specific conditions attached for different types of events. If you are organising an event in premises with an existing entertainment licence, you will need to familiarise yourself with its specific requirements.

43 Public entertainment licences do not replace the need for you to comply with the provisions of the HSW Act. The HSW Act should not be confused with entertainment licensing, which is dealt with under separate legislation, such as the Local Government (Miscellaneous Provisions) Act 1982.[27]

44 If your event is, or may be, subject to licensing control, it is advisable to discuss the findings of your risk assessment with the local fire authority before putting your proposed fire safety measures into place. This can help you avoid unnecessary expenditure.

45 If you already have a licence, you should discuss your proposals for changes to the fire precautions with the local fire authority before approaching the authority who issued your licence.

People with special needs

46 Legislation dealing with people with special needs makes no specific requirements regarding means of escape. However, the Disability Discrimination Act 1995[28] requires you to make 'reasonable adjustments' to ensure that no person present is at a disadvantage. This includes ensuring that people with special needs can leave the event safely in an emergency.

47 You should therefore ensure that your emergency plan takes account of people with special needs. You should identify the special needs of any disabled employees when planning your emergency arrangements and evacuation procedures. You must also consider other less able-bodied people who may have access to the event.

48 You have to bear in mind the difficulties experienced in entering and leaving the event, particularly in an emergency, by people with various physical and/or mental disabilities.

49 If any of your employees have disabilities, you should consult them about your emergency plan, taking their disabilities into account.

References

1   *Health and Safety at Work etc Act 1974*
Ch 37 The Stationery Office 1974
ISBN 0 10 543774 3

2   *Management of health and safety at work.
Management of Health and Safety at Work
Regulations 1999: Approved Code of Practice*
L21 (Second edition) HSE Books 2000
ISBN 0 7176 2488 9

3   *The event safety guide: A guide to health,
safety and welfare at music and similar events*
HSG195 HSE Books 1999 ISBN 0 7176 2453 6

4   *Guide to safety at sports grounds*
('The green guide') The Stationery Office
ISBN 0 11 300095 2

5   *Five steps to risk assessment: A step by step
guide to a safer and healthier workplace* INDG163
HSE Books 1998 Single copies free, multiple
copies in priced packs ISBN 0 7176 0904 9

6   *Safety signs and signals. Health and Safety
(Safety Signs and Signals) Regulations 1996.
Guidance on Regulation*s L64 HSE Books
1997 ISBN 0 7176 0870 0

7   *Fairgrounds and amusement parks:
Guidance on safe practice* HSG175 HSE Books
1998 ISBN 0 7176 1174 4

8   *Working together on firework displays:
A guide to safety for firework display organisers
and operators* HSG123 HSE Books 1999
ISBN 0 7176 2478 1

9   *Health and safety at motor sport events:
A guide for employers and organisers* HSG112
HSE Books 1999 ISBN 0 7176 0705 4

10   *General COSHH ACOP (Control of
substances hazardous to health) and
Carcinogens ACOP (Control of carcinogenic
substances) and Biological agents ACOP
(Control of biological agents). Control of
Substances Hazardous to Health Regulations
1999. Approved Codes of Practice* L5
HSE Books 1999 ISBN 0 7176 1670 3

11   *Temporary demountable structures:
Guidance on procurement, design and use*
Institute of Structural Engineers 1995
(Available from 11 Upper Belgrave Street,
London SW1X 8BH)

12   *Bombs: Protecting people and property*
Home Office 1999 (Only available on website:
www.homeoffice.gov.uk)

13   *Managing health and safety: Five steps to
success* INDG275 HSE Books 1998
(Free leaflet)

14   *Fire Precautions (Workplace) Regulations
1997* SI 1997/1840 The Stationery Office
1997 ISBN 0 11 064738 6

15   *First aid at work. The Health and Safety
(First-Aid) Regulations 1981. Approved Code
of Practice and Guidance* L74 HSE Books
1997 ISBN 0 7176 1050 0